HORSE DANCE UNDERWATER

HORSE DANCE UNDERWATER

poems
Helena Mesa

imagination series #13
Cleveland State University Poetry Center
Cleveland, Ohio

ISBN 9781880834824

First edition
5   4   3   2   1

This book is a title in the imagination series
published by the Cleveland State University
Poetry Center, 2121 Euclid Avenue, Cleveland OH
44115-2214.

Book design by BookMatters, Berkeley
Set in Joanna and Gill Sans
Cover design by Amy Freels

Library of Congress Cataloging-in-Publication Data

Mesa, Helena, 1972–
Horse dance underwater : poems / by Helena Mesa
        p.   cm. — (Imagination series ; #13)
ISBN 978-1-880834-82-4 (acid-free paper)
    1. Cleveland State University. Poetry Center.
II. Title.   III. Series.

PS3613.E7886H67   2009
811'.6—dc22   2008054544

ACKNOWLEDGMENTS

Grateful acknowledgment to the editors of the following journals, in which the following poems appeared, some in different form or under separate title:

Barn Owl Review:	"Apologia for Dating a Marxist"
Barrow Street:	"Tilt-a-Whirl of Our Untelling"
Bat City Review:	"Notes on a Saint: Deirdre, Brigid of Munster"
Cream City Review	from "Brevity of Snow": "Brevity" "Interlude" "Unstoppled" "Yesterday"
Diner:	"Everything Beautiful, or Not"
Ekphrasis:	"Returning to the National Gallery of Art to See *Rue des Moulins: The Medical Inspection*"
Fourteen Hills:	"*Gusano*"
Full Circle:	"Small Spaces"
Indiana Review:	"Braids of Water Too Swollen to Bear"
Pleiades:	"Mechanics of Early Autumn" "Reason"
Third Coast:	"Magnolias, Falling" "The Yaw"
Zone 3:	"The Art of Storytelling" "Sway This Night" "Tonight, No Sleep"

I am grateful to all my teachers for their guidance and generosity—thank you. Special thanks to Miah Arnold, David

Bernardy, Daniel Blasi, Danit Brown, Lisa D. Chávez, Stephanie Dern, Blas Falconer, Jessica Grant-Bundschuh, Antonio Jocson, Beth Martinelli, Marc McKee, Melissa Mercer-Tachick, Daryl Murphy, Glenn Perusek, Michelle Provorny, Amy Terstriep, Erin Walper, and June Yang.

I am indebted to Michael Dumanis, Rita Grabowski, and the staff at Cleveland State—this book would not be possible without their insight. Thanks to the University of Maryland, University of Houston, Writers in the Schools, and Inprint Foundation for their support. Lastly, my sincerest gratitude to my family, especially my parents and sisters, for their faith, for their encouragement.

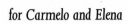

for Carmelo and Elena

Hearing the wren sing and falling cease
And bowing not knowing to what

—W.S. MERWIN
"For the Anniversary of My Death"

CONTENTS

HORSE DANCE UNDERWATER

Prologue to Lost

Like woods with a steel-toothed trap
under all autumn's lost leaves,

your god is always savage—
in one version white heat,

in another, scarlet, too gone to remember
so you delude yourself with lights

keeping the moon off scrapers, black sky
off the earth, its streets signed *Do not enter*

slumping you in a café
swollen with unfamiliar shadows,

waiters carrying trays of tea lights
in glass eyes, thin haloes of grace.

Years ago the church bells dropped
their tongues, but soon you tell time

by the weight of vertebrae
and stars, always those stars you track

hoping the world will stop
when you look around, to breathe,

to trace each moment before
it's gone. Maybe then it will burn

clear and bright, maybe. Except
then there's something else

given up, though it stays, and desire
for that stay traps like a coal mine.

If Zola wrote that the horse could never leave
the mines, lowered in as a foal

to be buried within sooty tunnels,
then what is this to us? What more than

small humans, crouched behind a tree,
peeing, while the canoe club waits in earshot?

What more than an orange vest loose around your chest,
because with years of lessons at the Y,

you can't swim? There is always a girl
standing in a halo of streetlamps,

alone in the silence of a cul-de-sac, late
when all meals are eaten, TVs cold and dark;

if that girl were to close her eyes and linger,
the world might grow around her, a sacred grove

she could almost reach and touch.

Cabin Fever and a Sliver of Light

Sky full of passenger pigeons, so many
their flapping thunders, leaving the heart stark,
nothing offered in the midst of so many wings.

Light fails, as if buried in a cave, its mouth
plugged with a stone larger than the moon
and what can anyone offer when rage grows,
stretches really, like beaded elastic

strung around your neck. Kneel inside
long hours, the ground will swirl,
wind warble like a violin string snapped

vibrating in third or fourth dimensions
you hear but don't understand. If someone
offers to cut a hole above, drop a sturdy rope,
a kayak rope, and pull you through,

know enough isn't—
sound fevers mid-day, mid-run, mid-bite,
mid-sentence, a theme song

that leaves you sleepless, the night
mute in such darkness
with one window open, above,
snow dusting your crown, shoulders

and the wonder, if these cold
brushes could sustain. If the road
could ever be cleared, if only, just enough.

Sway This Night

It reminds me of departure, this town
gutted with rails and passing trains whose horns
insist we waste our nights. At four, darkness
numbs our hands, hollows the streets
except for those trains, and after, a stillness
no one wants. My first autumn, then winter,
I began to believe I knew each train
by sound—silver bullet with a dining car,
freight of longhorns, and second to last, hogs.
It went this way. Each named by the drag of steel
on steel that says, This night belongs to no one
but me, named in the boredom that comes without
love, and the belief that the conductor speeds home
to something, until my chemist friend explained
that every few years in these boxed-up towns,
someone lies across the tracks after last call
before the sky melts like beeswax, the stillness
a wisp of air like madness in fear. No more,
no more. Even the wind pressed off the sides
pushes back, its metal cold, like the loss of breath
after a blow. The body stands, sways, in wait.

Notes on a Saint: Deirdre, Brigid of Munster

d. 570

So tranquil, she let a beetle devour her side;
townsmen said it grew hog-sized and roamed
the halls in fear of her steady gaze. After
they walked wide circles around her house,
the path a grooved orbit. She wrote letters
to her mother: *An animal sleeps in my mind,*
fur thick and mangled, then stuffed the notes
inside her mattress. Townsmen said she lived
on manna, though at night her abdomen
puffed with air and tree sap, a round hump.
In the spring they brought her the blind:
two parents, a priest. She could do more, they knew,
left stones outside her door: three smooth offers
for something taken and missed. *Is it real?*
Will it ever wake? A girl asked if her hands
bled at night, if they tasted of iron stakes—her eyes
wistful, as only a girl's could be, her stink
dumb, like sour milk. She told the girl to leave,
walk until she could no farther, and settle, there,
a true penance. *It curls tighter. To breathe,*
a chore. For days the river fought its banks,
the air was a broth. Leaves shook rain
and as she waited for the drops to burn her veil,
fireflies dawned, their light a mortal light
that left her dizzy and sick, the animal large and foul.

Gusano

n. a worm; a traitor; a Cuban émigré

It starts with the paper: Boat Sinks After
Deporting, he read; none of the crew
survive, although they found a trunk
charred & shored along the morning rift.
It starts with blue fire, the heat
deep in his bones, spreading to lungs
filled with hornets. Skies were charcoal
beds left to die of their own accord;
when he walked beneath, he was sure
no one watched—shadows were shadows,
breeze simply a breeze, & bending trees
swept his path of fearful signs. It starts
with a giving up, brief, a gull
alighting for bits of paper & cigarette butts,
its flight to sea grown farther & farther;
starts with letters sent without stamps,
& the room suddenly clear: hot water
in the pipes next door, weight of a book
settling into itself, rustle of stems
like a slow guitar; starts with stained hands,
ink that burned like thread wound too tight
around his left thumb. It starts before he knew
it had begun—the cold surging outside
unknowable, an illness that struck
familiar, insatiable,
a clatter of words, & the loss they stood for.

Apologia for Dating a Marxist

We bet on horses, stuffed
stubs in our pockets, each brush
brief while the pack raced by

until, gripping my shoulders,
he leaned in, the crowd unseen,
and kissed. It was his edge—

black leather slouch, stare,
tongue burning like vodka
that drew me. Call it *blasphemy*

or *betrayal* or *memory lapse*
even *defiance*. What you said
was *escape*. You left Havana

with 50 bucks stashed in a soap bar
and a box of tobacco for trade,
the boat full of nuns and priests,

and after it docked in Spain,
the boat caught fire and sank.
In my making of the drama,

I saw two weeks in hiding
on a dusty couch, curtains
closed, saw a fatigued man

stamp papers by rote, your
back no longer straight.
We believed we were right,

a plant unearthed, dragged
indoors, forgetting what
lives with it, how red ants

line tan buds. Time passes
and it has nothing to do
with anything but the taste
for more, a long slow burn.

Stasis at Fifteen

Mid-August, a steady heat hemlocks.
Boats float on water too deep for crabbing
and when you dive, ripples broaden
but the boats remain still. In the distance a radio
cites today's news, same as yesterday—
another hijacked tourist, another heat record.
What's changed? At eight, the want to flee?
At ten, the restlessness for something else?

Dusk, row to the canal's mouth where
stillness ends in a darkness too large
for hands to steer. There, salt laps the air,
a gauze rag that scratches cheeks and gags
the buoys' clangs. Stop. Tie down each oar.
What you want will come, swallow you whole.

Braids of Water Too Swollen to Bear

Outside the fort's walls
their ships leer, and we so few,
husbands fallen like white flags
waiting for a breeze. The timid
bishop stops at shutters, calls
though no call is needed.
Sash untied, hair loose, I wrap
rags to the ends of old brooms
while my sister lights the torch.
She hears the ships creak, says
she hears young soldiers clean
their rifles, the sounds like gates
unlocking; she sees the boat's ribs
from leagues below, and there
the current bats her back and forth.
If only her sway could curl the sea
into one tidy wave. If only night
released its will and skinned
the sky of every silver scale.
We march. Down blue bricks
to the plaza, we pray and march
to Ursula. What madness to ask
a woman long dead and distant
for help when neither ill
nor dying. Soon, morning hours
scar our postures with thoughts
of how we're still awake, how

raw words could change a war.
Our chants hoarsen and against
a ceiba some stretch, their candles
cupped close to their chests.
Girls spin and spin and spin,
their winged hands flapping
another girl's skirt, until she
spins and spins, the flames
too swollen to bear. Another
machetes a coco and slips it
between my hands, but the sweet
water couldn't coat a dry throat.
I shoulder my sister's arm.
I'd like to tell her the footsteps
are heartbeats, Ursula's, nearby,
I'd like to tell her pink light
softens harsh intent,
that the ships will be gone by dawn,
something good, lovely even
but the promise is a
braid of water, heavy and cold.

Tonight, No Sleep

Phone rings at three a.m., and yes
on other nights I'd be angry

at a dead line, a heavy breather
or an Italian operator asking me

to accept the charge, but tonight
is different. The line hangs:

A chin chafes the mouthpiece.
A throat clears: *Dad died.*

If I had a brother, I'd think
it were him ready to break

but I've never heard this voice before.
I should forget this man until morning

when I call my father. Worried
his lilies need rain, he'll ask

the forecast, as if knowing of the drought
could save the dirt beds.

How comfort from such distance?
This sky, this stranger's same sky

with its slighted light of winter stars,
begs to hold the line. One slip

and I'm an intruder without words
for his grief. No storm builds,

no cello dusks the heart. He is alone,
his face a stone without eyes, mouth.

Mechanics of Early Autumn

Migrant workers pick late tomatoes,
the rows half-tidy, the last before the men
pack and move on, leaving beehives
half-fallen from a tractor, combs empty.
Lilac fails yellowing grass. Steeples finger
the hammocked sky, insignificant rebellions
you would say, simple details like cracks in a mug
cast as sadness. Glaze cracks, china chips,
the day is not unraveling. And still
on the drive, leaves raise their silver hems
to walk through puddles not yet formed.

According to Hollywood, Every Word Said
Over Radio, Television, Phone Orbits Earth

Again, turn the car key, watch six men
drink beer on a distant porch—their words
slap their palms, and you hope they don't
hear the starter scrape, metal on metal.
Tweed sticks to your thighs, wipers drag
while yards back, the flooded road stands smug.
Back when we pressed cups to our ears,
waited for words to travel scraps of yarn,
what we imagined frayed into silence—
crickets, raindrops, yes, but words, rush of
sound, no, until the other child—a boy? girl?—
just needed to hear something. When one
of the men raps a fist against the window,
says, *Pop the hood*, you fear the glass's rattle,
the knuckles, the sureness in his spread legs.
One by one they come, nod something
you don't know but dread. Outside now
you stand—the rain persists—
wrench and wires in hand, saying *y'all* and *nah*,
cutting speech, stitching time, like kids do
when they know the con and want to disappear.
Earlier that morning: a different stranger
hunched against a glass wall, and spoke
softly through a phone. His words lacked force
as if the hospital room were a vacuum
that drew each syllable, then shot

each into the atmosphere beyond. His bed
pushed to the wall, the triangular space, the mask . . .
You pity him, like pity now belts your fender
to another stranger's pickup. *Hold steady,*
yield to no one. Something but nothing happened.
At your house they unstrap the strap, leave the car
teetering on a ditch. They depart. Rain still
pings, something you hope means more than
sound, more than the babble of *No, no,* the words
suspended underwater, no, tethered to the ground.

The Yaw

Three feet ahead, path dark except for her flashlight's bob,
she walks into the new year. Trees rise off the Indian trail,
reach for something beyond, and listen. You follow
the smallness your hand once traced—her spine, nape
pressed close. Now, crunch of snow beneath boots
and wind stealing under pants, between
scarf and bare neck. Each stone her steps kick back
you heard as a nocturne, but now—
the song that plays, if she were present or not—
what does smallness matter? What if landscape is memory
seen without its hemming leaves? Limbs creaking, ice
    breaking.
What if this is all there ever is to give?

Reason

. . . by rain and need, by the weight of what momentarily is.
—JACK GILBERT

The closest is a cello.

The closer the bare hand, the more pressure, the less song
to dampen what isn't said on the long drive home.
He said a deer crashed through the law firm window
and died. Right where he'd sat.

And I wanted to hold him, grip that cello's neck
and crush its frame. Snap wires, splinter wood.
But I said nothing. Or more likely, mouthed *Jesus*
to air, stagnant and humid and hot. Again

silence is a cathedral door
carved with spirals and suns, so heavy with age
it's impossible to pull open, though the beyond is familiar
coolness that might offer relief, if not belief

that inside the moment isn't yet
a malformed moment, another deer
splayed on the side of the road, or even two
grazing in the field you now pass. *Here,*

little moment, here-here, little moment—
If I jangle a treat will you leap into our laps?
Stretch and curl, the leash slack,
or snap and snarl at each passing car?

Returning to the National Gallery to See
Rue des Moulins: The Medical Inspection

to Henri de Toulouse-Lautrec

Dress hiked-up, ass bare, this gal
will parade before clients at the sixth brothel
down the street, but for now, she waits,

the walls a sick orange, her silhouette
a question before a man, barely seen,
turned in disinterest. Where I stand

you sat, drawing her with charcoal,
only to paint the sight later. Strange
how we jot scenes to remember

what we never say or show—to the left
is the unseen: the doctor waiting
to inspect, to say, no rouge, plumed hat

or leg-of-mutton sleeves will save her
even in your sketch. Even in this museum
where a guard ignores her blotched face,

I hide what I most fear: I bring nothing
to this dim room, a Sunday packed
with visitors and loud shuffles which stop

to complain of the banging down the hall—
construction. We could be on a torn street,
atomized with noise expected the night before,

a New Year's when I hid in a one-room
apartment, under blankets, and held a man
in this cold city. Perhaps that's why

I return, not for you, but for chaos
and some relief to chaos, the two
together, an edge between. We think

all is lost if we're bold enough
to move forward, all is lost if we hesitate
as if fearing what one might think

of our vision or the touch that remains.
A friend once told me the story of a fireman
who pulled a stranger from the wreckage,

and when he laid the man on the ground,
the man whispered, "Please, hold me a bit longer.
No one's held me in years." And for once

the story turns heroic—or is it dangerous?—
the fireman stayed with him, held him.
Why is it so difficult to consider
the gestures as real? That anyone would?

Notes on a Saint: Lydwine of Schiedam

d. 1433

After a boy pushed her from behind. An ice rink, 1396.

The sky purpled behind the scrapes of skates
along the canal, still looping in twists and turns
of flirtation—whomever a girl mittened or boy poked
through woolen shirts and coats. Her fall braced
too late—the rib broken, the voice heard
not the boy's *sorry* sweeping her hair. Carried home
to drawn shades and snuffed candles, the remaining light
crackled through the room, a squall of snow
dusting the shoulders and femurs of the house.
Her fever cracked and spit. She thought she heard
the murmurs of prayers lull and still, so the dead
lost their way. What did she see in the sullen spirits
perched in her small yard? What she saw or couldn't
and later missed went on around her—light near gone,
arm near numb, the yard a river passing unseen.

Galvanism

Years back, the projector's tsk tsk
woke us to screens of cells pulled apart,
a gurgled battlefield, though we knew blood
pumped louder, felt it fever our tongues
at the wake; its taste unhinged,
dressed us in black skirts and heels
clicking in defeat. Her body found,
a hummingbird stilled, and found.

The pressure of weight, wind and ice
can suspend a steel bridge,
                              and a blade
bleed organs, stain tees, blame a boy's hand
for blackness, nothing more.

To understand, we stole words,
chanted until we slept, believed
waking a sudden jolt, like old Galvani
shocking frogs until the corpses
convulsed—our senses would clear,
wiser than before. But it was only
darkness waking in darkness,
grass damp and cold, space walled
by bushes, car lights flickering between
houses, and the thought:
                              Someone might
pass, someone might notice the bed

empty, backdoor unlocked, hear a pulse
beat too slow. This darkness, this night
she never slept through, this waking
finds her alone, knowing the last loneliness
is a shallow shadow, moments before—

Transcript

Donora, Halloween, 1948

What we stood beneath and within was punishment,
god-style. The air inverted and trapped the smog,
a sick yellow, near black, a betrayal we sensed and saw
but didn't understand. To stretch an arm was to erase

its hand. Like those costumes
darting in and out of sight from the parade—
tail of a demon child, gone, a majorette
afraid to toss her baton, gone, the ruffle of skirt. . . .

Only noon, and we marched against the distant whistle
marking the afternoon shift. The plant hummed on.
Later, a neighbor would rasp truck tires along the curb
to find his way home, a daughter would flee,

breath held against the restive world
like graffiti promises she knows won't keep: John + Shane
forever. The words swayed, small dandelions of light,
tricks of time and space spliced and wound—

the brown fields, the unseen sky, the need to believe
those brown fields still lay beyond the darkness,
the sky above would pull the fog up and beyond the valley,
and the air would forgive what the rain could not.

The Art of Storytelling

The story goes like this:
A woman with blonde hair
to her ass rides
the back of a motorcycle.

This appeals to me,
the nerve, the fervor,
the ability to ride anything
in darkness, on slick streets.

That blue jeans girl
in a leather coat wraps
her arms around a man
whose face I can't see

and his heel snaps back,
his hands rev the engine
and they pull away
from a dumpster. This

is when my mind shutters
closed. *Someone stops them,*
I don't know who.
How say?—*They douse*

her hair with gasoline.
How explain
the dark figures, how they
step back, light a match.

Transmissions

A woman chatters about her lack of love
on the radio screwed to the cheap nightstand,
but at five a.m. her Southern rasp
is better than dreams where nothing moves—

I'd rather listen to this stranger
keeping company as she reads:
. . . *because you exist and because*
you don't, and this happens to everyone—

but the novice loses her caller, and
dead air leaks over radio waves
like the moment after a hurricane—
air electric, leaves motionless,

birds and wind stalled.
                              Somewhere, someone
does not exist, so the station transmits
recorded sound. All night the booth stands
empty, and the world sinks a little like

how that host explained string theory, said,
if you tear space, it fills itself like quicksand
rushing into itself after the body sinks.
Once, nooked in a near-stranger's arms

after three sleepless nights,
we listened to hockey, the emcee
naming men and moves and scores,
fluid grace in his voice, blind need

to pass the solitude of night—
we gripped without words, one inside
the other—it might seem real,

             it might—

Mechanics of a Self-Portrait

Winter, a child rode to school, alone,
wore a navy peacoat, and to say cold
cut through blankets, tamed city nights
is to say speech is invention that cracks
leather seats, swirled white between
letters dressed as elephants and snakes.

For years a thin girl pet her knee
in a cab where no one spoke, even now
circling the park, two words
snow the river and closed bridge.

Water rushes. Geese crap the lawn.
Two women with sea kayaks holler
as they shove off, then the stillness
meant to resist, except for Sundays—
taught to honor something, she chapels
her mind for an hour or so—Hush, hush.

Songless

The way we fear tragedy and can't stop.
Night tars the road, fills with *soon*
we'll all be screwed. Escape

is dramatic in rain, lit by an inn's bauble-
glow for the lost. We ate like animals.
With faith we watched wind sweep

clouds from the ridge, the end close
after weeks living from a bag, after years
living the way we do. Forget light

passing through windows and streets,
our need for light to wake us from sleep,
push us through. We never speak

splayed on a beach, trashy book in hand.
It's on mountain roads far from home.
It's alone, knowing someone nearby

grips the bed. Mouth dry and open,
asking to tread somewhere holy, untouched,
and for a moment, asking

to rise over that damn ridge.

Small Spaces

You want to be elsewhere, but stand near
nurses in yellow masks and paper boots
a few feet from the body, face down
on the gurney. Its sheets fold to expose

the lower back's valley, an open window
in which the surgeon slips the thick needle,
twists, removes the marrow, then reaches
for another. Shudder against the wall

full of spigots and dials. A clock tells
the wrong time, then the heart skips its beat
and when it stops, there's no turning back.
The body radiates pale light into the room,

it is the field agape beyond the glass,
the bird soaring then wanting,
when does it end? The want for someone
to cup your face in his palm, and say, *Hold on,*

you are here, but even then you can't believe
love will outwit the earth's plea to come home.

Absence Sheds Its Color

She loved the brush of an arm
but only when snow misled the day.

Before, her mother ushered children.
She thought they waited
near the refuge, their backpacks damp,
mouths snapping like small gulls.

Let grace be the absence of madness
and madness be the absence of all lies.

Back then she never thought she would live
like this, her wrists tied with biting rope, the rope
another decade of loss. One hot air balloon
red above the car scarring this desert.

One red moon in the night.
Two snuffed fires, the hearth black, black.

The Rafters: Key West, 1994

There sits this raft, *La Balsa*. So close
to *basta!* enough! Cobbled from black inner tubes
like the ones you might bob in on slow rivers,

bound to blue tarps to keep dry. All these
pass that unmarked mark, thin line
drawn on the mapped Atlantic. Cuba. Florida.

It's like play between siblings lying
too close. And on that site, exiles anchor
rented fishing boats, nets hanging, in wait,

the numbers too great for the stubborn
Coast Guard to stop, as if anyone could.
A woman leans forth at the stern, her arm

stretched to sailors watchful in the distance,
their figures small in the swaying flotilla.
Where's the waving flag? White headscarf?

Ninety miles never seemed so far—
such stories, recent as they are, fade
in the water's lap against rubber. . . .

At The Schooner, a tourist bar,
collages lace *Welcome* with curled rope
and wind chimes along the jetty's neck:

there, a woman comes upon it—
where she would straddle slick rocks to fish,
feet ankle-deep—the black tube

she's seen in the news for weeks. She pulls
the loose rope, heaves dead weight to a path
graveled with fish scales, hooks, wire,

signs of all who have come and gone.

Roadside Steakhouse

Near Houston I saw this peacock swing,
her bustier purple and black, and pinned to her ass,
feathers: starched, dyed, even tucked in her curls.
She clutched thick ropes, crossed her ankles
like a child might—thirty feet above us—then pumped,
head flung back, her laughter a heavy thought,
the thrill of a heel sliding up her leg not unreal.
Knives scraped plates, the tables too close,
waiters trayed blocks of cheese, war-era, the T-bones
ribbons of abandoned fat. There were stag heads
nailed against ochre newsprint, and outlines
of divas snaked in boas, all cleavage. On stage
a man played, it seemed, until he half-turned,
his gloved hands two crows, hovering, the song
a susurrus in the room's rush. Forgive me:
I wanted her to lean farther—blonde mane sweeping—
fall and fall and never land: finally she would be
something else. For sometimes grief appears
as rage, for sometimes we cannot change the rest.
We paid and left. A caddie pulled from the lot,
its exhaust thick as ether. Across the way
The Pink Pussycat glowed, its asphalt shimmery,
the broken glass like sequins, a merciful lawn to lie on.

Horse Dance Underwater

This has nothing to do with grace,
only slaughter and intense heat,
flies, and from behind, a *Don't look*.
No bones, no blood, but amber manes
inside the tannery. Our guide
hands us mint, little leafy sprigs
for shit stippled along the path,
flesh baked too long under the sun.
In casks, in chemical green, boys
ride a chestnut's back. Its skin
bobs, from its neck, from its girth,
haunches, legs—flat, like bed sheets
laundered with those swimming
boys. Without thought, they sing
Marco, Polo. They call in Arabic
and I mishear *Marco, Polo*,
charms for the beholder, against
boys pushing the next life. Beyond
the tanner's walls, camels roam.
One, its hump tall as the horizon,
breaks from the pack, parts its lips.
Soon olive branches will seed,
the desert will pull its reins tight
so the leather blisters. Pray wind
lifts the din of boys, splashing.
Pray we learn to look back.

Nor'easter

Naked, he ran to the water and back,
snow thick between the shag rug and lake
and his *oohs* soft, as not to wake

his mother. Next morning, we scaled
the fence, ripping my jacket, then landed
palms first on the old side, what he'd said

was once a blacks-only beach, back before
white blinded the roads more, like this storm,
snow not falling, but belting our torsos,

swings hidden, shore a thin sheet of ice
and then I knew he'd leave, desire
a gaggle of thoughts soon silenced,

but we're not there yet—We don't always
know what we know until it's late
and the tea kettle wails a little, and he says

your name, first time that month,
then it's all sleep, winter thoughtless,
tossing salty grays like a wounded thug,

and you, too dumb to know better,
you think the jacket is nothing, a tear,
one you can stitch in a bold color

because you believe the sky is constant,
a sign, like now, this new storm.
It's not that the past is the past,

but that each time we return,
we feel the past for what it was. Who we were
à la Psych 101, your voice girlish,

suddenly vulnerable, you who
crack stones, not to find fire, or bruise,
but in the clack, the cleft, a bloom.

Magnolias, Falling

for Megan

No portly moon. No beacon for that
silver-black night, she drove the snow-
blurred road toward the radio, her song
stalled by the mountain and its static,

her few words faltered until the skid,
two streaks raked into darkness. Outside
the cracked window, blossoms snowed,
chilled her body amid glass and ice.

She reached. Reached for the tree,
her arms numb, heavy. Driving now
this radio song suddenly reminds me—
her books on Homer, her room's small space.

We mocked the tango's turned face,
walked the quick slide, knees brushing thighs,
hands a tight clasp. A few strands of blonde
clung to her lip; I brushed it back.

Once, crouched low, her fingers
two horns on her head, she shouted,
Tatanka! before she told me the latest
peace treaties, how the war wouldn't last.

Ten years later the body is still
just a body. A magnolia falls, touches
the earth. And the vision of this night enters
into the next and the next and the next.

Everything Beautiful, or Not

Because Stelarc pierced his back with 18 fishhooks
and pullied himself between two apartment buildings
to prove *Everything beautiful occurs when the body
is suspended*. His back shaven, his flesh a naked ridge
of tents tied to ropes pulled through rings, his arms free
to swim above his quiet spectators—who believed

what they saw? Because neither a radio broadcast playing
Ramón Raquello and his orchestra's dance music
interrupted by reports of gas eruptions off Mars
nor a rocket with a *curious humming sound* could ever
send a city into alarum again, and because war
is now a barge of lights and sounds that buoys the waves

between a satellite and the living room TV. Because
when cleaning the fishbowl, the dirty water rushed
down the drain, and Rico, beautiful Rico, slipped
through cupped fingers into the garbage disposal.
Fished from the blades, the blue boomerang survived
half a day. Because when asked to read a poem,

my student, a flirt at twelve, claims he's an illiterate,
then laughs. He asked, *Why write?* and I choked.
How explain silence? How in dreams words appear
as Sanskrit? And because my student's friend couldn't stand
the feel of a pencil in his hand, and I did not wrap
the No. 2 in rabbit fur, nor tell them Whitman published

his first column at age twelve. Because two artists lived,
harnessed by a stretch of rope for a year, and never
    touched,
near the end, never spoke. One slept late, the other jogged
in place. One reached for pinecones, the other stalled.
Two branches bending their backs to a cord grown taut.
Because I don't know what beauty is, I compromised

what I saw, didn't see. I know Australian scientists
teleported a speck of light; I know the plane's departure
and arrival isn't always an end, but abhor it anyway;
I know the closest to an eagle in flight for the first time
is a Beechcraft propeller because I have been caught
in its soar, my knuckles white from gripping the earth.

The Prophecy of Red

after Henri Matisse's Red Studio, *1911*

i.

Look, Ford began the assembly line,
Rutherford formulated his theory
for atomic nuclei, there was a revolution
in China, the Italians defeated the Turks,
the Mexicans revolted, and Matisse

painted the room stark red, violent,
a red that's difficult to manufacture
but nature gives readily
like a seductive bird, persistent, invasive. . . .

So furious it spills over itself,
reproduces energy from nothing
in a way physics cannot explain.
How possible the world seemed,
the parts not given, but made.

ii.

Embassies bombed, and we turn,
shrug *What happened?*
but track the latest storm patterns,
news reports: *Fires sweep Mexico,*

stay indoors. Northern winds
choke the air with ash
masking the city's face.

No warning ever stops
the runners stepping outside,
lungs expanding like billows,
bodies stretched skyward in belief—
The sky will break and offer rain.

A Pebble Held Under Tongue

Street's wild, drumming
not unlike birds caught
inside a cupola. Cars bend

the turn, each one
your name, each sight lost
before loss ever understood.

A woman mopeds past,
singing, her voice the helm
of what's known,

trinket of time no one wants
to wear, and yet, we do.
The bike's light bobs

and the road seems to shake,
a nervous hand, as it writes
again and again, *please*.

To Drive Along a Road of Deer

Una candida cerva sopra l'erba . . .
—PETRARCH

Tractors strip fields of wheat, the hazing dust
like flies in flames. I should watch for them,
a mother and her two, three, but this moon won't
allow, a porcelain bowl so full the mind falters;
its light cracks fields, same light that hunts
darkness through mazes of wheat before wheat
bows to blades. Deer cross to streams, and there
in the current, they return to what they were:

deer, crazed by light, pawing, huffing at a man
anchored on the bank. Anything else pales—
ghostly, chewing-on-cheeks and longing for what
is not. This thing is not a she fleeing
into thick woods, this thing is illusion—
mud-slipping-feet-, splashed-water-, bruised-knee-
illusion. Let the white moon taunt and taunt
for what cannot be caught, for what cannot be.

The morning after

the baptism, hair and skin salty with sex and sand,
two boys arrive, crack open beer
and scour what's left behind.
They're sure it's along the beach
grieving the night passed, filled with empties
and cigarette butts. They're smug,
know they'll find the way in ways I never was.

Isn't that why I stayed? For some
guide to the now? For luck I gave up,
let the water take me, first my back's arc
then neck then crown until I slipped
lower than I meant, into scarves
of sea wrapping around arms and breasts,
silk that kicked my hair into ocean fans
and slunk between my legs; I rose for breath
alone in the midst of close friends

and teens, hundreds of teens
enfolded, mouths roaming, tongues desperate.
One pair fucked two feet away, chest-deep
in kelp and soft moans. Nothing kept
from holding back or from giving in
to the body—the beach so close, solid terrain
a short lurch away. There, no one dared sink
into arms and hands, or trust their weight
in the unknown that props
from behind, or the quiet lie:
There's no fear in letting water prove
you can surface, whole, howling and alive.

Brevity of Snow

Santiago, Chile: 1983

1. BREVITY

Remember how much you loved and stop there:

Brilliant gray hung on the field where boys played soccer.
A Pacific wind swept the hillside in wide circles,
cut through the schoolroom where you sat in your cotton
    coat
reading *Don Quixote*. The teacher closed her book.
She said, *Something is coming*. Outside students gathered,
their faces open to the sky, their arms like windmills.

A light snow fell,
the city's first in ten years.

Stop there, in the fading light.
Amidst their ringing voices.

2. UNSTOPPLED

That first time,
perched by the fireplace,
math book open,

your face burned dry, back iced
from the room's dark affront.
In bed, fleas nested,

left unasked-for marks,
small insistent wounds.
Another scratch on raked legs.

Upstairs a dubbed movie,
its voices murmured down.
Fire spat, a log fell.

What you thought: A plane
passing overhead
came without warning.

The house quaked. Roof
tiles shook. The bomb's
echo rose and fell

stalled by the Andes.
The city settled in
silence and fog before

dogs barked, neighbors
banged pots and pans.
For days that sound

and you, held by thunder,
mufflers, engine revs,
unsure if its aftershock

would strike again,
if the earth were a house
ready to crack.

3. INTERLUDE

Crowds, the chance to disappear like smoke.
The pleasure of childhood, to slip from sight
like a folded map slid under the car's seat
when the city roads are familiar. Billboards,
train tracks, a left at the bread shop, the theater,
right at the gas station—the path to a stable
where trainers amble home from apple orchards.
You long to ride there, alone, on Jack Daniels,
the horse whose hoof missteps, his canter off.
The two of you for miles. The trees hide
the city, its cars, blares, and everything within.

4. LETTER HOME

Voices woke me. I thought
morning understood its light
for a moment. The sky dawned

midnight, a strange glow.
"Roofs afire," translated
down the street and wind.

My sisters, I imagined, stood
close, weighed a blanket
on my shoulders, its threads

pricked my neck, but the hands
were strangers. The sounds
stacked like boxes around us.

Bells rung, not for church,
not for praise, and smoke
choked the bewitching light

of the horizon. For once,
the journey didn't matter.
All this was before,

maybe after
their voices woke me
from down the hall: too loud,

too drunk, past curfew.
The city's? The house's?
What does it matter

how it began?
At the field's edge
milled a crowd, unsure

how the world spit
such fire, how one spark
tore chaos from the earth

and sprang forward,
how a house could hold
the lives inside if the walls

were screens of smoke,
if the lives are nowhere
to be found. My sisters
were nowhere to be found.

5. INTERLUDE

Lights slowly ford houses and shops,
lampposts and sky. For what

should a child ask? What more
than lights blossoming into salvos

streaking the windows into psalms
for yesterday, a vigil for tomorrow?

Eleven, you knew nothing of truth.
It seemed simple. To think lights

travel miles of countryside for you,
and the ones beside you, those

at work, those at home. To think—

6. YESTERDAY

The hardest hour to see isn't always the darkest.
Dusk, and the world rives in two,
the seen and missed. Between them,

you repeat the story in a voice that smolders.
The Andes, faint behind clouds, reappear
like a white ring circling the morning.
Bags half-packed, you sat in a metal chair,
stomping the stage. The thuds echoed—
on the bus, in the fog, through asphalt and shovels,
by the roadside of that unbearable winter.
You were born whole, now your leg,
full of fear, shakes your hips, torso, and hands.
It will last only as long as you let—
let the fires die, clear rubble from fields,
line streets with paper lanterns. Strangers banged
pots and pans with wooden spoons, first
behind curtained windows, then candled yards, then
they were neighbors in crowds. The echoes wore
brick and stone. They called for water.
They rang the bells. They swept the ash away.

Mechanics of Unrest

A friend said he awoke
kneeling in a driveway,
skin bare and cold, mouth full
of small stones. The distant foundry
burned the sky black, or did the sky
snuff the town of all light?

Spitting the grit from his teeth,
he longed to lie beside himself,
whisper, *Hush now,*
but the lost hours called like mockingbirds

as when we try to make sense of
what is, what was,
and arrive at an orchard:

Against a tree, a ladder leans
slightly crooked, its rungs
disappearing in tufts of fruit,
bitter and tough. Inside
isn't sweet rain. As birds don't

blacken the sky,
the towards, not from,
irrelevant. As in, we want
what is to mean what is,
though what surrounds us
cracks and spits.

Nothing delicate
in disbelief, nothing

delicate in the wait
or distance between
an orchard and a field of stones.

A man awoke in a driveway,
mouth full of gravel, and at first
the moment seemed a joke, but
what if he wanted more than what sleep
gives, until the body took him
through the front doors, down the drive
barefoot on gravel, each stone
unfelt, until the body filled him
with whatever it could find, whatever
might be, filled him until he was full.

Tilt-a-Whirl of Our Untelling

. . . testimonio de lo que no decimos.
Reunimos nuestro tiempo, nuestros dolores,
nuestros ojos, las manos que tuvimos,
los corazones que ensayamos.
—JAIME SABINES

Because the cemetery gates were locked, you slipped your girl-frame through loose bars, only to rehearse the worst. Lift the player's needle or that song will cage the moment in reels of walking backwards between gravestones, looking out for rabid dogs on the way home. The ice-sky flashes. Birds pray, open-mouthed, flocked warnings of what's to come, a hell to all. But nothing came. Afraid to cross the street, that girl waited an hour for her mother. Want her. Want insides hidden like honeysuckle. Want that ailing posture you can't shed. That girl burned a matchbook on the basement floor, then buried the ashy remains with daddy's mums. Her too. Light will map a past. Go, gather it with the others: The one who crawled through an attic, kicked the ladder, and hid in a car parked by the madhouse until morning scarfed her in silk. The one who left on a boat full of nuns and priests and disembarked hours before the boat caught fire, and sank. The world tilts in strange guises. Behold these, love these.

NOTES

"Transmissions" owes gratitude to an episode of Terry
Gross's *Fresh Air*, heard on National Public Radio, and two
lines from Pablo Neruda.

"To Drive Along a Road of Deer" references Petrarch's
"Sonnet 190: Una candida cerva sopra l'erba" ("A white
doe on the grass").

"Tilt-a-Whirl of Our Untelling" quotes Jaime Sabines's
prologue to *Tarumba*, which Philip Levine translates as:
". . . a testimony of our untelling. / We gather our time
and our grief, / our eyes, the hands we once had, / the
hearts we rehearsed."

RECENT CLEVELAND STATE UNIVERSITY POETRY CENTER TITLES

Nin Andrews. *The Book of Orgasms*

Patrick Michael Finn. *A Martyr for Suzy Kosasovich*

Diane Gilliam Fisher. *One of Everything*

Susan Grimm, ed. *Ordering the Storm:* How to Put Together a Book of Poems

Linda Lee Harper. *Kiss, Kiss*

Jayson Iwen. *A Momentary Jokebook*

Sarah Kennedy. *Double Exposure*

Jesse Lee Kercheval. *Brazil*

Helena Mesa. *Horse Dance Underwater*

Henri Michaux. *Someone Wants to Steal My Name*

Bern Mulvey. *The Fat Sheep Everyone Wants*

Deirdre O'Connor. *Before the Blue Hour*

Barbara Presnell. *Piece Work*

Mary Quade. *Guide to Native Beasts*

Tim Seibles. *Buffalo Head Solos*

Tim Seibles. *Hammerlock*

Mathias Svalina. *Destruction Myth*

Allison Titus. *Sum of Every Lost Ship*

Kathleen Wakefield. *Snaketown*

Liz Waldner. *Trust*

Allison Benis White. *Self-Portrait with Crayon*

Eliot Khalil Wilson. *The Saint of Letting Small Fish Go*

Sam Witt. *Sunflower Brother*